What is toothpaste made of?

Disney BOOKS BY MAIL

When Mickey Wonders Why, he searches out
the answers with a little
help from these friendly experts:

Vice President and Publisher Cathryn Clark Girard
Director, Product Development Kristina Jorgensen
Editorial Director Lisa Ann Marsoli

DK Direct Limited

Managing Art Editor Eljay Crompton
Senior Editor Rosemary McCormick
Writer Alexandra Parsons
Illustrators The Alvin White Studios and Richard Manning
Designers Wayne Blades, Veneta Bullen, Richard Clemson,
Sarah Goodwin, Diane Klein, Sonia Whillock

Contents

What are baseballs made of?

First a little ball of cork is wrapped in a rubber shell. Then a handful of thick woolen yarn is wrapped around the rubber and that is held in place with a layer of cotton thread. The final outer layer is made of white leather, which is hand-stitched with thread.

Batter up!
Most major league baseball bats are made of wood. The barrel of the bat has to be perfectly round.

Inside story
Here are all the parts
that go into a baseball.
A baseball weighs
about 5 ounces.

Play ball!

☞ More than two hundred
years ago, the early settlers
played an English ball
game called rounders. This
is probably how baseball
began.

☞ Thousands of years ago, in
Mexico, people played a
game just like basketball.
They called it
pok-ta-pok.

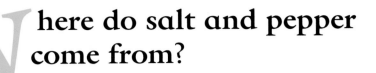

Where do salt and pepper come from?

Salt comes from the sea and under the ground. Pepper comes from the berries of the pepper vine that grows in hot places like the Caribbean.

Pickled pepper

 Try saying this very quickly: Peter Piper picked a peck of pickled peppers. If Peter Piper picked a peck of pickled peppers, where's the peck of pickled peppers Peter Piper picked?

Pass the salt
Salt water flows into huge salt pans. When the sea water dries up, it leaves the salt behind. As well as regular salt grains, people sometimes put rock salt on their food. Rock salt looks like white crystal.

Pepper, please!
The dried berries of the pepper vine are crushed into powder, or grains, to make pepper.

What is toothpaste made of?

Many different things. It contains chalk powder to polish teeth, foamy detergents to clean them, and a chemical called fluoride to keep teeth strong. It also has a sticky gel, usually made from seaweed, to keep the paste together, flavored oils to make it taste nice, and disinfectants to kill germs.

How does the paste get in the tube?
Through the bottom! The lids are screwed on, then the empty tubes go into a machine that fills them up with toothpaste and seals the ends.

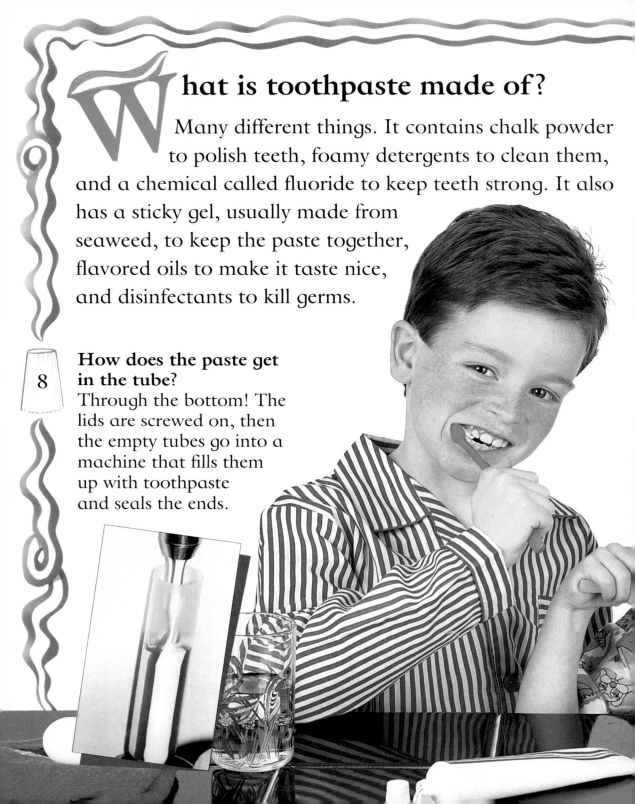

Teeth cleaning facts

Before people had toothbrushes and toothpaste, they cleaned their teeth in different ways. They used toothpowders made from burnt eggshells or crushed coral, and they used a rag to rub the powder on their teeth.

How is paper made?

Most paper is made from trees. Logs are chopped into woodchips. The chips are then mixed with chemicals and water and turned into a mush called wood pulp. The soggy pulp is put into a machine which spreads the mixture onto a moving belt. Huge rollers squeeze water from the pulp and flatten it, and hot rollers dry it. And then, out of the end of the machine comes a new roll of paper.

Recycled paper
Old, used paper can be made into new paper, called recycled paper. Recycled paper is a good idea because it helps save trees.

Making money

The paper for making dollar bills isn't made out of wood fibers, but out of cotton rags. That's because the fibers in cotton are stronger than the fibers in wood.

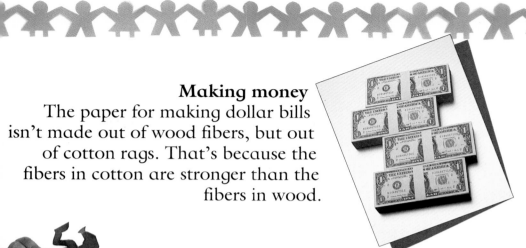

Here's your change
"Doctor, I keep thinking I'm a dollar bill!"
"Go shopping, the change will do you good!"

Paper facts

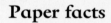 Some forests are grown especially to be made into paper.

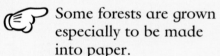 The first people to make paper from pulp were the Chinese. They made paper from bamboo.

The queen wasp chews wood to make pulp, and then makes a papery nest with it.

How are the paints in my paint box made?

The paints in a paint box are usually watercolors. They are made out of different things such as ground-up colored earth, rocks, and dyes – and then mixed with a gum to hold it all together.

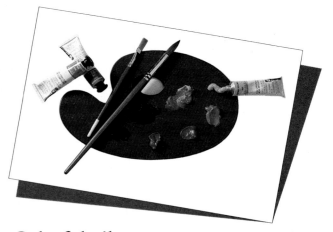

Colorful oils

Oil paints are usually made from the same things as water paints, but oil is used instead of water to hold the paint on the paper or canvas. Oil paints dry much more slowly than water paints.

Picture perfect

☞ Portraits are pictures of people.

☞ Landscapes are pictures of places.

☞ Still lifes are close-up pictures of everyday objects, like fruit.

How is glass made?

Glass is made from sand, a chemical called sodium, and limestone. They are all heated together in a very hot fire until they turn into liquid. The liquid is then cooled a little, and air is blown through it to shape it into things like bottles, jars, and glasses. Machines in factories shape the glass but sometimes people do it by hand.

Special glass
Some people are especially trained to make wonderful glass shapes. They are called glass blowers.

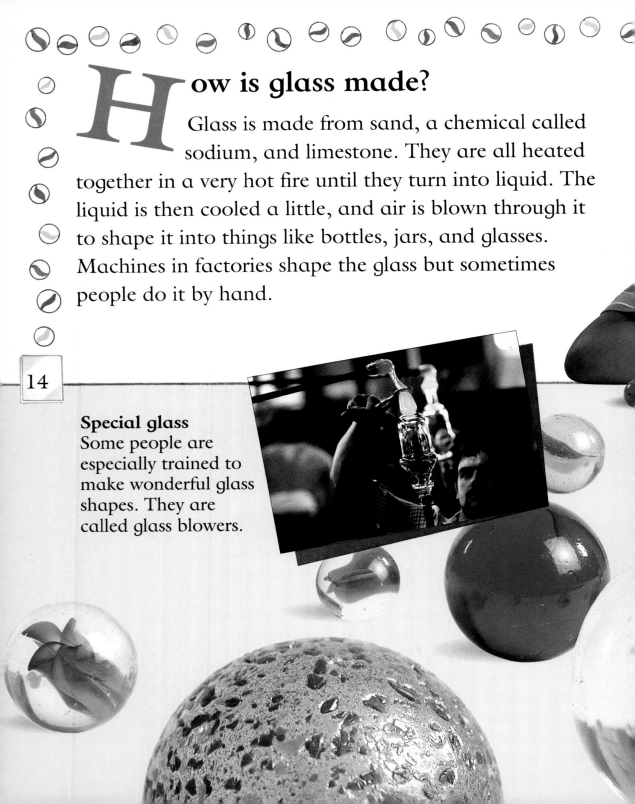

See-through facts

Different chemicals are added to the hot liquid to color the glass.

The first glass things known, were beads made from rough lumps of glass. That was 4,000 years ago in Asia.

How are pencils made?

Just like a sandwich. You start with two large slices of wood. Each slice has grooves cut into it. Next comes the filling. The filling is made from a soft rock called graphite. It is cut into long, thin sticks and placed in each groove, on the bottom slice of wood. The top slice is spread with glue and put on top. The "pencil sandwich" then goes into a machine that cuts, shapes and paints each pencil.

Before pencils
Children didn't always have pencils and paper to write with. They once wrote on slateboards, or blackboards, with chalk instead.

Feathered pens
Years ago, birds' feathers were used as ink pens. They are called quills. The sharp tip of the feather was dipped in ink.

Write this down!

☞ The first people to use pencils were the ancient Greeks. Their pencils were flat cakes of real lead, which is a metal.

☞ More than 10 billion pencils are made each year in the world.

How is ice cream made?

Cream, eggs, sugar, and flavorings are mixed together and then frozen. While the mixture is freezing, it is stirred to keep it smooth and creamy, and to stop chunks of ice from forming!

Teddy bear sundae
Would you like to make a tasty dessert? Put three scoops of ice cream in a line. Use fruit for the eyes and nose, chocolate for the mouth, and a banana for the arms and legs.

What a chore!

This is an old-fashioned ice - cream maker. Inside is a bowl which sits on crushed ice. A paddle fits into the bowl, and when someone turns the handle, the paddle stirs the ingredients.

Scrumptious ice-cream facts

☞ Ice cream as we know it today was first made on the island of Sicily, just off the coast of southern Italy.

☞ The world's first ice-cream factory was built in America in 1865.

19

Where do clothes come from?

Factories! The cloth to make our clothes is made from thread. (Threads are thin pieces of twisted fibers.) The threads are woven together to make sheets of cloth. The cloth is then dyed and sometimes printed with patterns. At another factory, the cloth is cut and sewn to make clothes. Then the clothes go to stores, so we can walk in and buy them!

20

Natural fibers

Until a hundred years ago, most fibers came from plants or animals. This is a silkworm – it makes silk. Fibers from plants or animals are called natural fibers.

Funny, ha, ha!
When is a chair like a piece of material?
When it is satin!

Modern fibers

In the past 100 years people have discovered how to make new kinds of fibers, like polyester. These are called manmade fibers. It's hard to imagine, but your bathing suit is probably made from oil, coal, or wood!

All dressed up

☞ Clothes have been worn for thousands of years. People first wore clothes to protect themselves against the weather, or to decorate themselves.

☞ Some of the earliest cloth was made out of tree bark.

How is chocolate made?

It is made from the beans of the cocoa tree, which grows in the hot, steamy rain forests of South America and Africa. The beans are picked and sent to factories. There they are toasted in large ovens to bring out their flavor. Then the beans are squashed and turned into a thick liquid, called cocoa mass. Sugar and milk are sometimes added to make the chocolate sweeter.

Delicious fun!
What's huge, brown, and
tastes delicious?
A chocolate dinosaur.

Inside the chocolate factory

The chocolate mix is sent to candy factories where it is turned into all kinds of tasty delights. Machines shape the candy, and people check that the machines do the job properly. They even get to taste the candy as well!

Chocolate facts

 The first people to enjoy chocolate were the Aztec people of Mexico. They mixed the ground-up beans to make a thick, bitter, frothy drink called chocolatl.

After the Spanish arrived in Mexico, they took the idea of chocolate drinks back to Europe. They added sugar and vanilla to make them sweeter.

How does soap clean things?

Soap is made up of millions of tiny parts called molecules. Each molecule has a head and a tail. The head likes water and the tail likes dirt. The soap molecules surround the pieces of dirt with their tails sticking into the dirt, and their heads into the water. This loosens the dirt, and it floats off into the water, leaving your clothes nice and clean!

What is soap made of?

It's made of fats, or oils, and chemicals. Soap also has perfume in it to make it smell nice, and dyes to make it look pretty.

Clean facts

 Soap doesn't always come in bars. It also comes in flakes, grains, and liquids.

Long ago, before soap factories, people made their own soap by boiling fats with wood ash. The soap cleaned well but it was gray, gritty, and it smelled pretty bad.

What are cups and saucers made of

A special, stiff mud called clay which can be shaped into different things such as cups and saucers, plates and bowls. After the pieces have been shaped, they are baked until they are hard and dry in a special oven, called a kiln. Most cups and saucers are made in large factories, but some are still made by hand.

26

Factory pots
In factories where they make plates, cups, and saucers, the clay is shaped in molds. That way they can make lots of items that look the same.

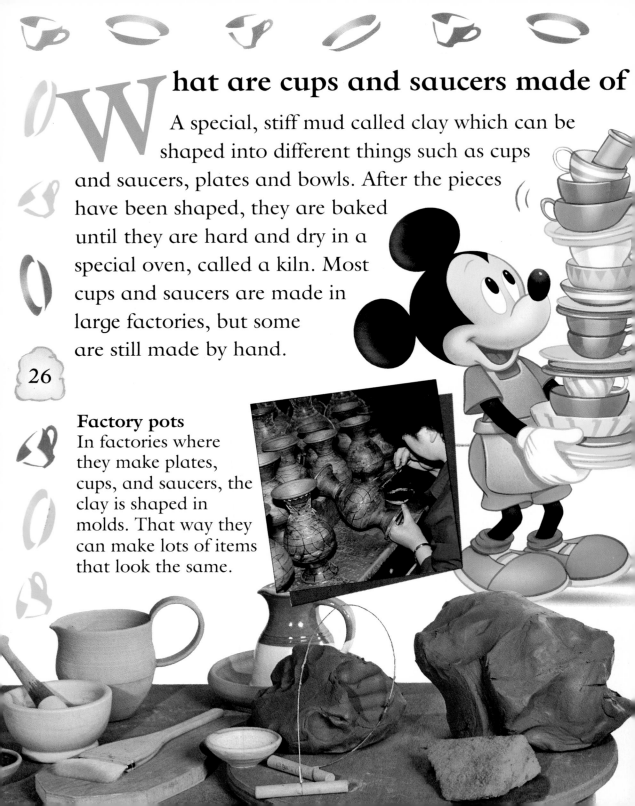

Clay facts

☞ Pots are among the very first things that people learned how to make. In museums you can see pieces of bowls and cooking pots that are more than 5,000 years old.

☞ Bricks are also made of clay and cooked in a kiln.

Spin off!
Some things such as bowls and vases are made by hand on a machine called a potter's wheel. The wheel spins around while the person shapes the clay.

MICKEY'S Mind teaser

The pictures below complete each sentence. Can you tell which picture belongs to which sentence?

1. Pencils are made from _____ .
2. You need some _____ to make ice cream.
3. One place that salt comes from is the _____ .
4. Cups and saucers are made out of _____ .
5. Chocolate starts out as _____ .

1.

2.

3.

4.

5.

Mickey Bonus: Can you write the missing words?

1.Wood 2.Cream 3.Ocean 4.Clay 5.Cocoa beans